I0011329

Blockchain Blueprint

*The Complete Guide to Blockchain Technology
and How it is Creating a Revolution*

Ray Toffler

Table of Contents

© **Copyright 2017 by Ray Toffler**

All rights reserved.

The following eBook is reproduced below with the goal of providing information, that is as accurate and as reliable as possible. Regardless, purchasing this eBook can be seen as consent to the fact that both the publisher and the author of this book are in no way experts on the topics discussed within, and that any recommendations or suggestions made herein are for entertainment purposes only. Professionals should be consulted as needed before undertaking any of the action endorsed herein.

This declaration is deemed fair and valid by both the American Bar Association and the Committee of Publishers Association and is legally binding throughout the United States.

Furthermore, the transmission, duplication or reproduction of any of the following work, including precise information, will be considered an illegal act, irrespective whether it is done electronically or in print. The legality extends to creating a secondary or tertiary copy of the work or a recorded copy and is only allowed with express written consent of the Publisher. All additional rights are reserved.

The information in the following pages is broadly considered to be a truthful and accurate account of facts, and as such any inattention, use or misuse of the information in question by the reader will render any resulting actions solely under their purview. There are no scenarios in which the publisher or the original author of this work can be in any fashion deemed liable for any hardship or damages that may befall them after undertaking information described herein.

Additionally, the information found on the following pages is intended for informational purposes only and should thus be considered, universal. As befitting its nature, the information presented is without assurance regarding its continued validity or interim quality. Trademarks that is mentioned are done without written consent and can in no way be considered an endorsement from the trademark holder.

Introduction

Congratulations on getting your personal copy of Blockchain Blueprint - The Complete Guide to Blockchain Technology and How it is Creating a Revolution. Thank you for doing so.

The following chapters will discuss everything, that you need to know about blockchain technology, if you ever want to consider yourself a source of knowledge within this field. We will start by discussing, why there was a societal need for blockchain technology in the first place, as well as go into some of the key companies that blockchain helped to create. These companies include Bitcoin and Ethereum. The concept of blockchain can be complicated if it's not properly broken down and discussed in small chunks. This book will make the concepts regarding blockchain technology accessible, and allow you to feel as if you have a clear understanding of what blockchain is, and how it can better the world.

You will discover why blockchain matters in today's society, as well as gather an understanding of how blockchain can be used in both the financial and non-financial sector. Of course, blockchain began through the financial platform of Bitcoin; however, today it is equally being considered to be used for non-financial endeavors such as determining contract ownership. When you begin to understand, that blockchain can potentially re-establish, how consumers interact with their marketplaces in a variety of ways, this will only enhance blockchain's importance in your eyes.

The last chapter will explore blockchain's implications for the future from an economic perspective. These days, this world is anything but certain, and everything seems to be constantly moving faster than it did yesterday. Blockchain has the potential to dominate the structures of our society in multiple ways, which means that our role as reactionary participant in the global marketplace has the chance to change. The implications of blockchain suggest that consumers should be more than passive bystanders throughout the purchasing transaction process. Through more transparency and more trust, blockchain technology is striving to change the way that individuals interact with their banking institutions.

There are plenty of books on this subject on the market, thanks again for choosing this one! Every effort was made to ensure it is full of as much useful information as possible. Please enjoy!

Chapter 1: The Big Banks, Consumer Trust, and the Notion of Decentralization

Up until 2008, large banking institutions were largely seen to be honest and transparent. While their motivations have always been about prioritizing a need to make money, the public eye at least interpreted banking activity as being fair (for the most part). After the events of 2008, all of that changed. With the economic crash of 2008 came great waves of fear, uncertainty, and anger that was directed towards the banks, who had deceived the public into thinking that the economy was expanding and flourishing at an unstoppable rate. In fact, the opposite was true. Basically, the banks and the mortgage companies had been giving people loans that they couldn't afford, so that these naive homeowners would spend their money and later be unable to sustain the large mortgage payments they had agreed to finance. The result was a spike in homes foreclosing across the country. This ultimately led to greater poverty, homelessness, loss of jobs, and civic unrest.

The 2008 housing crisis was not only a national phenomenon; it affected the entire globe. Even though the bank's deceptive nature had ultimately led to the global economic downturn, at the end of the day they hardly paid any consequence. The decision to release the banks from their responsibility in the manner and instead bail them out of their debt due to the foreclosures, that had occurred was one, that lead to even more civic unrest. The Occupy Wall Street movement is only one manifestation of this unrest; however, it's safe to say that many more people than the ones, who were publicly protesting felt, as if they had been deceived and cheated. This put the public into a unique and disturbing position. Feeling as if they had no other choice, most people ultimately continued to do business with their banks and brushed their dismay aside. This allowed and still continues to allow the banks to gouge the public financially via expensive fees associated with withdrawing money from ATMs, the high cost associated with late fees, and additional types of transaction costs. Most of the public swallowed this pill and played by the rules that the banks were setting; however, a tech-savvy minority was not going to sit back and watch as the banks swindled their way out of this financial crisis. They were ready to act, but they did not exactly know how, yet.

Since 2008, everyone can agree that the rise of the internet as a marketplace has grown tremendously in scope. Everyone wants to be in on the action of buying and selling products that can be delivered right to your door with only a click of a mouse. Of course, Amazon is continuously revolutionizing the way in which we perceive and interact with our online shopping experience, but there are websites of smaller scale that are also contributing to this mass gravitation towards online consumerism. These sites include EBay, Zazzle, and Grub Hub, just to name a few. Today, if you own your own business, it's almost a necessity for you to also have an online presence. Without one, the climate of today's marketplace will not be advantageous to you, and there's a greater chance of failure. It's as simple as that.

The problem with the gravitation towards online consumerism is that these online businesses still need to interact and work with banks, if they want to make money. Even though the credit card has become arguably more important than paper money, the company who issues the credit cards still plays a vital role in all transitionary processes. If we go back to the distrust that the 2008 economic crisis brought with it, online shopping does not alleviate any tension that still may be resonating from that event and events similar to it; however, the online marketplace does highlight a crucial element to our burgeoning technological society. On a mass scale, we seem to moving from a physical world into a digital world. The digital world does not have to be anything like the physical world, if we don't want it to be. The technology gurus of the world are continuing to shape the cyber realm as they see fit, whether or not these methods and procedures are similar to the physical models that preceded them. This is where we find ourselves in relation to blockchain technology, and society's roots of distrust with large banking institutions is a strong example of how the notion of blockchain ultimately came to be regarded as a highly viable option for the future of enterprises, that require consumer trust in order to run well.

In Blockchain We Trust

Blockchain can be seen as the answer to society's trust issue with the banks because of its peer-to-peer design. Instead of having to rely on a shady bank in order to complete a transaction on the internet, blockchain technology allows users to transparently see *all* of the transactions, that are taking place within the program's network. This eliminates any potential for secrecy or falsehood, because if one person notices that something is amiss, he or she can then alert everyone that something isn't right. Bitcoin was the first company to develop the notion of the blockchain. We will go into the specifics of both Bitcoin and blockchain's history and implementation in a subsequent chapter, but for now it's important to understand the service that Bitcoin was attempting to provide via blockchain. Rather than having a single private banking entity receive all of the financial information for a transaction (giving them the potential to manipulate it or use it in an unethical way), Bitcoin sought to promote a decentralized form of conducting financial transactions. Through cryptographic technology and a public space, where everyone can virtually access the entire financial network at any given time, Bitcoin was the first institution pursuing the larger goal of taking their trust away from the banks and instead putting it back into the hands of the people.

Trust Given to All

For Bitcoin specifically, in order for everyone on the network to be able to see the transactions that are going through the system, they developed what is known as a public ledger. This ledger documents every single transaction that takes place, and is distributed to every user on the network. Blockchain technology makes this possible. Through the development of Blockchain, Bitcoin made it possible to eliminate third-party participants such as large banking corporations. The ability to create a public ledger, that succinctly and chronologically categorizes all of Bitcoin's transactions is a staple of what blockchain can offer the world, all through the lens of being a trustworthy source of information. This may not seem like a huge feat, but to a society that has been using physical and concrete banking institutions since its origin, the construction of a completely digital bank is something that is certainly innovative.

It's important to understand that while Bitcoin is what made blockchain popular and accessible for others to use, Bitcoin itself is now considered to be less reliable than the blockchain technology that was created for it. Perhaps you have heard about how Bitcoin users have had their currency stolen in the past. If you have, it's important to note that these problems had to do with other aspects of the Bitcoin technology, problems that were separate from the capabilities of the blockchain. Today, it is widely known that blockchain technology can be used to help structure and secure multiple types of transactions, that are both financial and non-financial in nature. Because of the fact that blockchain technology originated through Bitcoin, it is important to understand how Bitcoin operates and functions; however, it is more important to understand the ins and outs of blockchain, because of the fact that blockchain has grown beyond its initial uses within Bitcoin.

Chapter 2: The Development of Bitcoin, Cryptography, and Public and Private Keys

Gaining insight into how Bitcoin works is the primary key to establishing a comprehensive understanding of Blockchain for two reasons. Firstly, Bitcoin is one of the most popular uses of the blockchain technology. Secondly, Bitcoin is a rather controversial use of blockchain for multiple reasons. One of the biggest reasons why Bitcoin is considered by many to be controversial is because it is the only type of online currency, that is not regulated by the government in some way, shape or form. Of course, from a public perspective this probably seems like a positive aspect of Bitcoin, because this means that the government cannot tax or infringe on an individual's ability to purchase and sell goods; however, there are safety factors that are in question because Bitcoin has to regulate its network autonomously. For example, what would happen if a criminal network were to start using Bitcoin as a legitimate way to funnel money to its members? The government would have no way to trace this money because it's being exchanged in an encrypted and unregulated way. Obviously, the crime organization in question would have to be quite smart in order to pull this off, but the possibility exists nonetheless.

Cryptography will also be discussed at length in this chapter, because the concepts of cryptography are essential to the functioning of the Bitcoin marketplace. Two other concepts that this chapter will also go over include public keys and private keys. All three of these concepts help to make Bitcoin secure, but it's primarily important to understand that this network would not be nearly as secure, if it were not for the blockchain methodology working behind it. If Bitcoin's network were not secured via blockchain, Bitcoin would run the risk of having their consumer's information hacked or used in illicit ways. After reading this chapter, it will more than likely become obvious to you as to why blockchain is important for not just Bitcoin, but for the entire internet community today.

Satoshi Nakamoto and the Development of Bitcoin

The notion of Bitcoin was developed by a man named Satoshi Nakamoto. In 2008 (the same year as the stock market crash and global economic crisis, mind you), Satoshi Nakamoto wrote an article that was titled, "Bitcoin: A Peer-To-Peer Electronic Cash System". During this same time period, the domain name "Bitcoin.org" was also bought from a hosting site. While it's impossible to tell whether or not, it was Satoshi Nakamoto, who bought the domain name himself. All we know is that in January of 2009, the first Bitcoin transaction was initiated. What's interesting about this Satoshi Nakamoto character is that there is very little knowledge of what happened to him after his article was written and the first Bitcoin transaction was completed. In fact, by 2011 it seemed as if Satoshi Nakamoto was nothing but a phantom, a distant apparition who introduced the world to Bitcoin before vanishing into thin air. This urban legend gets better. No one knows for sure who Satoshi Nakamoto was or is. This mystery lives on to the present day.

It may seem strange to you that the creator of Bitcoin himself seems to be a fake identity of some type, but when you take the time to think about it, his disappearance sort of works within the rest of Bitcoin's framework. If we think about the fact that Bitcoin was developed as a *decentralized* network, then this essentially means that no one can own it outright. With everything being transparent, a traditional business hierarchy completely vanishes. Of course, there are still people who work for Bitcoin and help it to operate its nodes (which we will discuss in the next chapter at great length), but it's important to understand that there is no "boss" or anyone, who is running the show outright. Had Satoshi Nakamoto created Bitcoin as "his" project, it would have taken away from the fact, that it is everyone's shared conglomeration. This is only a theory, but at least it can provide some insight into why a person, who created a new technology would be completely secretive and covert about its development.

Satoshi Nakamoto's article, "Bitcoin: A Peer-To-Peer Electronic Cash System" essentially outlined how Bitcoin functions and what it is. If you were to read Nakamoto's article, it would state that Bitcoin is an automated online currency exchange platform that can perform transactions without needing a third-party participant getting in the way of the transaction. The article places importance on the community members of Bitcoin, and the need for them to know about every single transaction, that is taking place on the forum. This way, there is consistency and transparency for everyone who is involved. Specifically, this allows users to concretely see where the finite amount of currency is moving and how much is being exchanged during a certain period of time. If we think back to the alleged disappearance of Satoshi Nakamoto, having him disappear rather than be the spokesperson for Bitcoin seems more reasonable. Had Satoshi Nakamoto kept his place as the leader of Bitcoin, the community-feel of the entire institution would diminish. Everyone would go to the leader when something went wrong, and the community as a whole would once again be hierarchal. Perhaps Satoshi Nakamoto's "disappearance" was more of an artistic expression against centralization than it was something entirely factual.

Understanding How Bitcoin Works through Cryptographic Principles

In the Bitcoin world, a "bitcoin" is a form of cryptocurrency. Cryptocurrency is a form of digital currency. Unlike types of physical currency such as the dollar or the nickel, a bitcoin does not have a specific value. Admittedly, this may be a difficult concept to wrap your head around, considering that currencies have only had a concrete value for your entire life. Instead of having a specific value, the owner of the bitcoin is able to give the bitcoin a value that corresponds to the value of the good or service that is being traded during a specific period of time. To put the value system of a bitcoin in perspective for you, it's important to understand how divisible a bitcoin is. A bitcoin is able to be divided into any amount of 100.000.000 units. This gives bitcoin users the opportunity to truly value their currency into boundless amounts. Additionally, the term "bitcoin" is not the same as the "dollar", in the sense that the origin for the bitcoin can be anywhere in the world and can change depending on who owns the currency and where they plan to trade it. For example, let's say that you have a dollar in your pocket. You end up flying to Iceland with this dollar in your pocket. When you get there, you go to coffee shop, reach into your pocket and take out your dollar. You go to use it to pay for the coffee, but the barista won't let you, because the Icelandic people do not operate with dollars, they operate with krona. This would mean that you'd have to go exchange your dollar for a krona at the going exchange rate before you were able to purchase anything in the Icelandic society.

With Bitcoin, you would never have to go through the hassle of exchanging one type of currency for another. Instead, you're able to give your bitcoin the value of a krona, and then easily trade with someone living in Iceland. With bitcoin, you are eliminating the need to go through the process of exchanging one type of currency for another type of currency. Instead, you are able to simply state what type of currency you want your bitcoin to be. Lastly, in addition to converting your bitcoin into multiple types of currency, you can also convert your bitcoin into units of energy, or it can represent stock in a certain company. This is an important aspect to understand about Bitcoin. The goal of the company was never to create a single currency that could be traded amongst different groups of people. Instead, Bitcoin is meant to be used as a way to preserve ownership of something, regardless of where you live or what the specific exchange rate is. Bitcoin, in this way, is able to represent a certification of digital ownership, and this goes beyond how traditional currency works because of the enhanced encryption methods that go into ensuring that an individual's currency is protected from intruders. As you can see, this works similar to a bank safe or safety deposit box, but it is more digital, transparent, and complicated to infiltrate.

Bitcoin and Cryptography

In Greek, the word "cryptos" means hidden or concealed. This is where the origin of the word cryptography began. Cryptocurrency, as we already defined previously is a form of digital currency; however, there is another aspect to it. In addition to being a form of digital currency, it is also online currency that must preserve its value through certain encryption procedures. These procedures are known as cryptography. Cryptography is a form of encryption that is used by private companies and government agencies alike. Instead of relying on third-party services to be "trustworthy" with confidential information, cryptography allows for complete security without the need for a human security representative. This eliminates any potential human interest that may arise regarding the information, and makes people feel as if their information is truly being protected. A key aspect of cryptography is that it requires the knowledge of certain types of information in order for the cryptographic lock to be broken. This means that if an intruder does not have the correct information, he or she is going to be denied access into the locked cryptographic portal. By requiring the owner to prove his or her identity, cryptography ensures that only authorized users are able to access the content behind it.

We will now take a look at four essential principles of cryptography. The purpose of cryptography is to uphold these principles as best as possible, so that no infractions occur and all information within a network is properly protected.

Cryptography Principle 1: Authentication

The first cryptographic principle at which we're going to look is authentication. The person who is receiving the information digitally and the person who is sending the information digitally must authenticate themselves, or in other words prove their true identities through cryptography. This isn't all that they must prove. They must also prove that the starting destination and the ending destination of the information are legitimate places, and that both the sender and receiver have access to these locations. Authentication in Bitcoin specifically, ensures that both the sender and the receiver are conducting transactions from trusted sources. This also helps to ensure that none of the information (or in this case, currency) has been stolen or obtained in some other illegal way. To put this in perspective, let's use an example. Let's say that you're looking to purchase an expensive purse (either for yourself or as a gift for a loved one). If you're paying full price, you're obviously going to want to make sure that the purse in question hasn't been stolen or is counterfeit. In order to make sure that the purse wasn't counterfeit, you could ask for a serial number or a location, where a database is kept of all the legitimate purses on the market for that particular brand. The principle of authentication for cryptography works similarly to this concept.

Cryptography Principle 2: Transparency

We have already talked about the concept of a public ledger, or a document that everyone receives within a blockchain system. A public ledger is an example of how a blockchain is able to achieve another principle of cryptography, which is transparency. Transparency makes it impossible for a person, who received or sent information to deny, that he or she ever sent it in the first place. If everyone within the network has a copy of the transaction that did indeed occur, then no single person has the ability to deny that the information was sent or received. This element of cryptography helps to build trust in the system and ensure that honesty is a priority. This prevents anyone within the network from trying to seize an unfair advantage. An example of transparency in the physical world could be as simple as a signature. A more complex example would be a notarized letter. When a letter is notarized, this means that a person was present at the time, when you signed the document. This ensures that what the signed document is saying is true, and this is transparent because of the signature of the other person who was present at the signing.

Cryptography Principle 3: Truthfulness

The third principle that cryptography seeks to uphold is truthfulness or honesty. This is similar to transparency, but it does not directly relate to the integrity of the network as a whole, which is what transparency is mostly referring to. Instead, truthfulness refers to the truthfulness of the information that is being exchanged within the network. Cryptography seeks to ensure that none of the information or currency being exchanged through the network has been altered or tampered with in some unauthorized way. For example, could you imagine, if you were performing a transaction on Bitcoin for $500, only to find that after you completed the transaction, you only received $250 for the goods. If this were to occur, it would implicate that there is a chance that someone altered your currency as it attempted to make its way to you via the person, who was originally sending it. Obviously, truthfulness and integrity of the goods or currency that are being exchanged is of utmost importance, especially when money is on the line. To put this into a physical example for you, a physical manifestation of truthfulness of a document or currency would be, if there was important information within a room, that required fingerprint access in order to enter. Only the people authorized with a fingerprint can access the information through the door, and they have presumably been vetted to ensure that they are not criminals or are looking to do harm to whatever is behind the locked door.

Cryptography Principle 4: Camouflage

The last cryptographic principle at which we're going to look is the idea of camouflaging the information being sent. When the information or currency is on the way to its final recipient, it would not be a good idea to show everyone on the network what is being exchanged. Of course, the final amounts that were received and sent can still be seen on the public ledger, but when the information is traveling to its destination, cryptography seeks to conceal this type of information. When the information that is being sent and received is concealed, it means that no one can hack into it or hijack the contents of it. A physical example of camouflage would be an animal, who is trying to get somewhere in broad daylight when there are hunters around. In order to get from one location to another, the animal will have to make sure that his or her identity is concealed. Otherwise, trouble or death could ensue.

The bottom line is that cryptography seeks to put trust into digital platforms, that can initially seem somewhat scary to use. Not everyone out there is well-versed at hacking or navigating the web, so they can rightly feel as if exchanging currency online is not a safe way to exchange currency.

Public and Private Keys

The last concepts that we are going to discuss in this chapter are public and private keys. Bitcoin uses private and public key cryptography in conjunction with one another, so it would be best to think about public and private keys working hand-in-hand. It is best to explain the concepts of the public key and the private key through Bitcoin, as this will be the most accessible way to understanding the concepts. Within bitcoin, every wallet in the network has a private key associated with it. It might be best to think of the private key as the DNA fingerprint, that exists for every single wallet within the bitcoin network. Without the wallet being activated and documented in the system, the wallet would not truly exist within bitcoin's network. If a user within the bitcoin network is looking to send or receive bitcoin into or from their wallet, they first have to authorize the transaction by using the private key, that is designated to their individual wallet. It's also important to understand that each person at opposite ends of the transaction are responsible for authorizing the transaction using their private key. This means that if only one person is interested in exchanging currency, the other person must also be in agreement. If only one person activates a transaction using their key but the other person does not, then the transaction will not occur.

Next, it's time to think about what the public key is and what it does. A good way to think about a public key is to consider it similar to a home address mailbox. When you have a home address, people are able to send you mail, but that does not mean that anyone else is allowed to open your mail without your permission. This is essentially the role of the public key. It's a way for others to find you, who are also on the network. Another way to think about how private key and public keys interact with one another is to think about male and female ends of a connector. Obviously, the male end of a connector is the part that sticks out, while a female connector contains the opening or is the connector that will receive the male one. The public and private keys work in a similar manner. In the case of cryptography, the private key would be the male connector, and the public key would be the female connector. In other words, the public key is going to receive the information from the private key. If we create an example for this concept, it might make it more accessible. Let's say that one bitcoin subscriber named Mary wants to send 10 bitcoins to another user named George. In order to do this, Mary would first send her private key to George's wallet. This would allow George to see that Mary does in fact have the 10 bitcoins that she claims to have in her possession. Her private key would be sent to George's public key, and then Brian could open it once he received it.

Once Mary sends her private key over to Brian's public key mailbox, she is essentially giving him permission to look inside of her wallet. Before George can see the contents of her wallet, he must first verify and confirm that he has received Mary's private key inside of his public key. This is purely for public ledger purposes. Now both Mary's wallet and George's wallet have verified that they are interacting with one another, and that they are content with the exchanges that are in the process of being made. It's important to understand that this process of verification shows the rest of the people, who are going to be looking at the ledger, that everything is as it should be between these two bitcoin participants. After George has verified, that he has received Mary's private key, it's time to look inside. Once again, George is making sure that there is sufficient coinage to cover an exchange of 10. After he is satisfied, George is able to accept the transaction, and it is deemed complete. There is no need for Mary to see George's private key, since he will not be giving Mary any of his own currency. Perhaps instead, he is providing her with a service or good that is more tangible in nature and Mary is paying him for this service or good via bitcoin. This makes sense. If you were paying someone for a service, would you demand to see their wallet before completing the transaction?

When Mary sends George her private key, there are two main things that are happening from a verification standpoint, that are important to bitcoin's overall security and cryptography system. These things are:

1. Mary's public key is able to verify her transaction history for George. When George is finally able to look inside of her private key, he may only see a number; however, he is able to cross reference this number with her activity on the public ledger. If Mary were to claim that she could give George 5,000 bitcoins but then her public ledger shows that she had recently traded 3,500 of her 5,000 bitcoins to another user, George can easily see that she does not have enough funds to complete the transaction.

2. When Mary sends her private key to George, she is essentially telling him that she owns this private key and public key address. If George were to receive the currency from another source that did not come from Mary's public address, then he would have reason to believe that the funds are either counterfeit or completely fake.

Once you understand how the public ledger works and the process between the public and private key, it becomes rather easy to discern how transactions occur within bitcoin. This process is largely straightforward, and this is intentional. If something goes awry or doesn't seem right, it is easy to identify because of the transparency of the network. We have discussed a lot of dense information in this chapter. Hopefully you will be able to make sense of it and unpack it in your head easily, because it only gets more detailed from here.

Chapter 3: How Blockchain Chronologically Fixed Bitcoin

Even though Bitcoin was able to create an environment, where people could send and receive information in a transparent and safe way, when they were first starting out, they were still having significant problems. This problem revolved around being able to put transactions, that occurred in Bitcoin in chronological order. If we go back to our previous example about George and Mary, this will make more sense. Even though we looked at the example about Mary and George, as if they were living in a vacuum, where only their single transaction was taking place, the reality is that within the bitcoin system, there are hundreds if not thousands of transactions taking place during a single period of time. This becomes a problem, when you try to put all of these transactions onto a clean and concise public ledger. The question becomes, which transaction goes on the ledger first? Let's say that in addition to George and Mary, there is also another two-people named Stacy and Stephanie, who are also completing a transaction at the same time as George and Mary. Both transactions complete at around 3:00 PM eastern standard time. Of course, this example may seem a tad coincidental; however, when you think about the fact that people all over the world have access to bitcoin, an even trickier question to answer is how will the public ledger deal with the issue of different time zones? This requires that the public ledger itself have an overarching standard for telling time, as well as a way to determine which transaction gets displayed first on the ledger.

The concept of a Blockchain was developed as a way to counter a problem that Bitcoin was having within its system. This problem involved putting the transactions in chronological order. Let's take our example from the previous chapter. While Emily and Brian are agreeing upon terms and finalizing their deal with one another, two people named Mary and Robert are also completing a transaction of a similar nature. It turns out that Emily, Brian, Mary, and Robert all finalize and submit their transactions at the exact same time, 2:03AM. This might initially seem extremely coincidental, but when you consider the breadth of Bitcoin and its worldwide reach, the possibility does not seem that unrealistic. The question for Bitcoin becomes, "which transaction gets recorded into the public ledger first?"

Changing how the public ledger operates helped to fix this problem. The public ledger documents what is being traded at a given time and is sent out to everyone within a network in order to maintain consistency in recordkeeping. Another way to look at this problem is to ask which transaction gets sent out to everyone else in Bitcoin first? If transactions are not put into chronological order, the ability for people to double-spend becomes even greater. For example, if you were looking to burglarize the system and sent one transaction at 2:03AM but this wasn't recorded until 5:04AM, it would look like you still owned currency that was actually already given away. To put this more simply, if multiple transactions are being made simultaneously, but are being recorded in a non-chronological way, the accounting of where Bitcoin is being distributed at any given second would be wrong. The public ledger would be wrong and people would not know exactly, who owns the Bitcoin in real-time. In this way, trust in the system would erode. The engineers at Bitcoin knew that they needed a solution to this problem, if they ever wanted their digital currency to explode in popularity. This is where the development of blockchain really comes into play.

All About Blockchain

To solve the problem of having to prioritize an order for multiple transactions, that happen at the exact same time, the first thing that Bitcoin decided to do was develop the concept of putting all transactions, that occur at the same time into what's known as a "block". You can probably see how blockchain ultimately got its name. As these blocks are created based on when transactions are made, all of the blocks are then linked together in a chronological manner. This means that blocks of information are also being recorded on the public ledger together. The information that is being recorded in a group fashion include the date and time, when the transaction took place, the name of the people who participated in the transaction, and the amount of cryptocurrency that is being exchanged between the two participants. As you can see, the idea to group transactions, that happen at the same time into a block largely eliminates the problem of how to categorize the transaction information on the public ledger; however, there are still plenty of questions that need answering. These questions include the following:

Question 1: How are the blocks along the blockchain being authorized? Who is giving the "okay" for these blocks to be produced?

Question 2: How can it be assured that the people, who are authorizing transactions along the blockchain are not corrupt themselves? How can the users of the bitcoin network be made to feel as if their transactions are being conducted by people who have integrity?

Both of these questions are crucial to the success of the blockchain. Failure to adequately develop methods that provide answers to these questions could have possibly resulted in the dismantling of Bitcoin. To compensate for these types of questions, the concept of the miner was presented.

Mining, Decentralization, and Nodes

We've already talked about this a bit in a previous chapter, but it needs to be reiterated. Blockchain as a system and technology promotes a decentralized way of controlling the ownership of something. Additionally, this idea is more formally known as the Distributed Consensus Model. In a centralized society, all of an individual's assets can be accessed within the walls of a bank. While this makes access to financial information relatively easy for someone, who is banking with only one financial institution, it's also important to understand that once someone's financial information has been given to a bank, this information is then accessed by a private entity. Of course, you will own your money, but the bank potentially can "work the system" to make money for themselves while they're holding your funds. This makes some people uneasy. When you think about the fact that many banks have locations across the entire country (if not across the entire world), it's pretty obvious that the big banks have access to a whole lot of money.

In order to keep track of this money, banks need people. These people are usually known as accountants. In the most basic sense, accountants spend their days calculating and crunching numbers to make sure, that the money coming into the bank matches the amount of money, that is leaving the bank. In other words, their job is to make sure, that the accounts receivable and the accounts payable match up with one another. It can be argued that, when you have people making calculations, there is more room for human error. Of course, these days it's likely that accountants are using computers in order to check the work that they're doing, but the potential for human error still exists. This method of a traditional bank system is different from the ideals of a blockchain. Sure, there are still physical people working within the system, but they are constantly being monitored and their work is always being standardized by computer algorithms along the path of the network. Let's get into more detail about how blockchain methods differ from traditional accounting methods.

Who Are These Illusive Miners?

Within blockchain, miners can be interpreted as taking the place of an accountant inside of a banking institution. A miner is the person, who essentially polices the blockchain network in the hopes of ensuring, that there are no counterfeit funds going into the network and that everything is running smoothly. Instead of going to an office or a place, where miners will police the entire blockchain system from a single location, these people are able to use their personal computers to achieve their policing objectives. This notion, that people can work together within a digital realm remotely, is not just decentralization at work; it's also distribution at work as well. By having people work in a variety of places, these miners are able to access different parts of the bitcoin network based on their location. Remember, Bitcoin is a global endeavor. It makes sense that miners can be located all over the world, and that these people do not need a "bitcoin computer" in order to police the blockchain. The advantages of being able to have people working for the blockchain via a personal computer are immense from an employment perspective. This means that a network that is on a blockchain can pay for less resources for their employees than they would otherwise be required to, if they have distinct blockchain offices. This is just one of the small advantages that a blockchain system can offer a company. Lastly, it's important to understand that within the Bitcoin network specifically, miners are compensated with small amounts of additional bitcoin currency. This provides sound incentive for the work that these miners are doing for the network as a whole.

The Concepts of Nodes

Now that you have a basic understanding of who the miners are in the blockchain and the role that they play, it's time to move onto the concept of a node. If you've ever taken a biology class at a point in your life before, then the term node might be ringing a bell in your head. If it's not, we can define it. Simply put, a node is a point of connection that facilitates a certain method of communication. When a particular network is comprised of mostly blocks, physical nodes can be seen along the chains of the network. "Physical" obviously implies that these nodes exist in some concrete form, and this is true. A physical node network system refers to the fact, that these nodes manifest themselves within a blockchain network via the presence of people sitting at computers that can access it. The people behind these computers are the miners, who are working to maintain the logistics of the network at any given period of time. These are the miners (as we've already discussed).

If we go back to our example of Mary and George, who are participating in transactions with one another, we already know that they are validating their transaction with one another via their private and public keys; however, the validation within this network of nodes goes beyond two users validating the existence of one another. In addition to George and Mary acknowledging their transaction, a message is also sent to every single miner along the entire length of the blockchain once the transaction has been completed. Think of this as being the equivalent of when you used to have to turn in a quiz and wait for a grade from a teacher. Until you know how you did on the quiz, your final grade is "pending" review. Waiting for all of the miners to review a particular transaction works in a similar manner. Before the transaction is uploaded and transmitted to everyone along the network, all of the miners must be in agreement that the conditions of the transaction make sense. This means that unless everyone is in agreement about the validity of the transaction, the transaction will not be posted. If one or two miners along the network decide that there is something false or fishy about the transaction, they are able to sound the alarm to the other miners for further investigation. As you can see, this is how the miners collectively can act like a policing force together, even when they are not actually in the same location as one another. Being able to collectively say whether or not a transaction makes sense provides a situation, where it is harder for someone to get into the system for hacking purposes.

The notion of miners acting like police vessels answers the two questions, that we identified earlier in this chapter. The miners are the ones, who are able to authorize transactions along the nodes of the network, and you are able to ascertain that they are not corrupt people, because if there was even one corrupt miner, the other miners within the network would notice that this miner is working in ways that are against the rest of the mining pack. By this point, you should have a working understanding of how the blockchain system protects the network, that it is supporting. Now that this has been established, we are going to go back to our original issue that Bitcoin was having. As a refresher, this problem had to do with figuring out, which transactions were going to be published on the public ledger first, and the solution to this was the idea of a block. If we dig deeper, it's obvious that there is potentially an additional issue that arises once the blocks have been created. This problem that needs answering is the following:

What happens when two blocks are submitted for publication at the same time?

This is an essential question, that bitcoin had to figure out, if it was going to successfully operate, and again the blockchain was able to come to the rescue. Obviously, in order for there to be a solution to this problem, there had to be some sort of prioritization standard set up along the blockchain. If there were no rules established about how the blocks were going to be ordered when two were submitted for publication at the same time, then there would be constant misrepresentation on the public ledger. The answer to this question has to do with the concepts surrounding hashes and nonce numbers. Let's take a look at these two essential concepts, and others, of blockchain now.

Prioritization Through Riddles

Of course, the problem of potentially having two transactions being posted to the network at the same time was solved through the development of blocks of transactions being grouped together, but you have now come to understand that this does not completely fix the problem. Along the nodes of the blockchain network are many miners, who are working quickly to have their blocks submitted. The faster a miner can submit a block, the quicker he or she can get paid, but what happens in a situation, where multiple blocks are submitted to the network at the same time? To fix this problem, the developers of the blockchain method had to think seriously about the notions of prioritization. In the end, they ultimately decided that prioritization needed to become a bit more complex and tricky. To solve the problem of multiple blocks being submitted to the ledger by the miners at the same time, the miners must work through algorithmic puzzles once they have a group of transactions ready to be created into a block. For an average miner, these puzzles require about ten minutes of time each. The next step to understanding blockchain is to understand, how these puzzles work and why they take ten minutes to complete.

Chapter 4: Hash Functions, Nonce Numbers, and Making Sense of it All

We already know that physical computer nodes exist along the chains of the blockchain, but there are other protective security measures, that exist along the chain as well. The first security measure at which we'll look is known as a hash. A hash services the blockchain by providing multiple functions of cryptography, including the following:

Hash Function 1: Verifies identifiers via two important hash functions (which we'll look at momentarily)

Hash Function 2: Helps to verify the public keys and addresses that are attached to each person's wallet within bitcoin

Hash Function 3: Ensures that the signatures of the clients who are using bitcoin are valid and true

Hash Function 4: Provide the blockchain with "proof of effort", meaning that the hash function ensures that each miner is doing his or her work properly

These four functions are the basic advantages, that hash functions can provide any blockchain network. You can think of a hash function as being a supplemental use of force in addition to a police brigade. This may mean that the hash function is similar to a S.W.A.T team or another form of enhanced weaponry (you can use your imagination). Understanding the functions of the hash functions can provide you with a better understanding of how the security within a blockchain network functions. As you can probably tell by now, there are multiple security tactics at work within a blockchain.

This allows for a multi-faceted approach to security. If for some crazy reason the private keys or the mining system were to go down, the hash functions would still be there to protect the system, and vice versa. It's important to note that, while there are other cryptographic security measures, that can be integrated into a blockchain, hashes are the ones that are most closely associated with bitcoin.

Let's take a look at the fourth hash function, the proof of work function. In addition to providing padded security for the blockchain network, a hash function also serves as a piece of the algorithmic puzzles, that we were talking about in regards to miners uploading blocks to the blockchain. Each miner has the responsibility of figuring out the hash function before the other miners in the network, if they want to upload their blocks to the network as quickly as possible. Remember, in addition to being compensated for the work that they're doing, these miners also receive additional bitcoins depending on whether or not they're moving faster than the other miners against whom they're competing. Rather than attempting to explain what the miners are doing with their hash functions, we are going to look at this process in a step-by-step fashion, so that it is more accessible. When we look at this process, we are going to assume, that the miner in question has already received multiple transactions and is getting ready to upload a block to the blockchain network.

Step 1 for a Miner: Prioritize the Individual Transactions

The first step that the miner is going to take after he or she has a group of transactions is chronologically order the group of transactions that came in to them. Yes, there might be multiple transactions, that occurred at the exact same time, but there may also be transactions that differ by merely seconds. It's the job of the miner to prioritize the transactions, and to do this, he or she is going to follow what's known as Little Endian sequencing. Little Endian number sequencing means, that the transactions are going to appear with the ones, that happened the most recently on the right, and the ones that happened later in time relative to the rest of the blockchain on the left. It's important to understand the Little-Endian number sequencing is the primary way that users on a blockchain are able to turn the individual transactions into meaningful information. In other words, Little Endian number sequencing is used as a type of language, that blockchain is able to understand, because the seemingly random numbers of a transaction are converted into a language, that the blockchain can understand.

Step 2 for a Miner: Input the Transactions into a Hash Function

While the Little-Endian sequence can help to standardize the transaction information for all of the miners, this does not mean that the sequence has been used for anything significant yet. After the miner has ordered the individual transactions, the next step is to input this information into a hash function. The hash function is what allows the transactions to be compared to other transactions, that are being completed by other miners within the network, and this is what is ultimately going to be submitted to be uploaded to the blockchain.

Step 3: Identifying the Hash Functions to Use

There are two primary hash functions within the bitcoin application that are used to process blockchain content. Remember Satoshi Nakamoto? The guy who wrote the original article on bitcoin and blockchain? Well, within that article were the two hash functions, that bitcoin uses that determines the order of what is uploaded to the blockchain.

They are as follows:

1st Hash Function: Hash160(d)=RIPEMD-160(SHA-256(d))

2nd Hash Function: Hash256(d)=SHA-256(SHA-256(d))

Admittedly, these two functions are a bit intimidating to look at, so let's unpack them a bit. Below is a list of variable terms that exist within this function. This list should be able to help you to figure out what goes where, if you were ever to try and input data into a function of this type:

Variable d: Variable d is a representation of the individual transactions that a miner is collecting and sequencing via the Little-Endian method. This number is obviously going to vary depending on the number of transactions that are being uploaded within the block and the size of the individual transactions themselves.

Variable SHA: Variable SHA is an acronym that stands for a Secure Hash Algorithm. Basically, the SHA is going to take the information that it's given and consolidate it into 256 bits. This means the 256 bits is its digest length.

Variable RIPEMD: This variable is also an acronym. It stands for Race Integrity Primitives Evaluation Message Digest. The digest length of this variable is smaller than the SHA variable at only 160 bits.

As you can see from both of the hash functions that are used within bitcoin, there is one that's been established for 160 bit solutions and 256 solutions. The miners know which ones they should be using for each transaction. The number that is produced once the hash function is figured out is known as a nonce. This is a miner's goal, to find a nonce via the hash function at their disposal. The nonce is the final product of the "proof of work" statement that the miner is looking to provide the blockchain community. This begs the question, what exactly is a nonce?

Defining the Term Nonce

A nonce is a number that has been generated at random and is only used once. This means that when a miner is looking to upload a block to the blockchain he or she is looking for a specific number from their hash function, that has been predetermined. Additionally, it's important to understand the hash function for the immediate blockchain in question is not the only one that the miner has to consider when finding the nonce number. In addition to figuring out the hash function for the current block in question, the miner also has to calculate the hash functions and find the nonce for the previous blocks of the chain. This process requires the miner to be doing multiple equations, and there's no guarantee, that the miner is going to figure out each equation on the first try. Now can you see why it typically takes a miner ten minutes to complete a single block of information? Add the fact that this miner is competing with other miners along the blockchain to figure out the equations first and as quickly as possible, and you've got yourself a situation, that is not entirely easy in nature. If it wasn't obvious before, it should be obvious now as to why miners get paid bitcoin to work for the Bitcoin network.

Bringing it All Together

The concepts and definitions that were presented in this chapter should now be able to work together in your head cohesively. Now that you understand, how the hash function works as a "proof of work" for the miners along the blockchain, you should be able to see how a blockchain ensures, that the principles of cryptography are upheld within a complex digital network such as it is in Bitcoin. These principles are upheld through the hash function, and are reinforced through the notion of the public and private key. An individual's private key allows him or her to feel safe as he or she conducts business with someone else within Bitcoin, and it can be argued, that individual users of bitcoin would feel less safe, if it weren't for the miners and the hash functions, that were there to police and validate the information, that is being presented as valid. Thus, the public and private keys, and the hash functions are working with the miners to ensure, that the honor of the entire blockchain system is kept intact. Hopefully, from reading this chapter, you have been able to ascertain that to some extent.

Specifically, some of the key points of this chapter include the fact, that a fraudulent miner is going to have a hard time counterfeiting results into the blockchain system for two reasons. Not only do all of the miners have to agree, before a transaction can be completed, but all of the miners also have to figure out specific and predetermined nonce numbers prior to having their content being considered legitimate. Additionally, this system is one, that is able to immediately figure out, when human error has occurred, and this arguably is better than a traditional third-party system of doing financial business. This allows for greater transparency and a greater sense of inclusiveness for all people, who are participating in the blockchain system, miners and basic users alike.

Chapter 5: The Problems with Bitcoin and Moving Beyond it via Fintech

For the majority of this book, we have been discussing blockchain as it pertains to bitcoin, primarily because of the fact that blockchain is where bitcoin originated. It's relatively straightforward to explain how blockchain technology works via the bitcoin application, but this does not mean that Bitcoin itself is as credible as the blockchain methodology. In fact, these days it is widely stated that blockchain is much more reliable than Bitcoin is for a variety of reasons. This being the case, it has become commonplace to say that blockchain is such a reliable form of programming that it has surpassed the capabilities of Bitcoin. This chapter is going to document some of the problems with Bitcoin, so that you can see how these problems are not associated with the blockchain method. Additionally, we will also look at how bitcoin opened up the door for other types of financial technology to emerge through analysis of the term fintech.

The Problems with Bitcoin

Although blockchain seems to be a sound type of programming methodology, the same cannot be said about the Bitcoin application. The biggest problem that Bitcoin faced, as of 2015 revolves around the idea, that they are growing at too fast of a rate. While it may at first seem like this is a "good" problem for bitcoin to have, because it implies that business for this company is growing, this is not the case because of the organization of Bitcoin from a network perspective. As it stands, Bitcoin can only process seven transactions per second. Of course, to many people this may seem like a lot of transactions, but when you consider the fact that the major credit card companies are able to handle much more than seven per second, this becomes a problem. The reason why Bitcoin is able to only accept seven transactions per second is because the current blocks along their blockchain are only able to process a certain number of transactions at a time. The developers of Bitcoin are certainly able to expand the capabilities of their blocks, but this would require every user of bitcoin to download a new network onto their computers. Additionally, the size of this operation begins to pose a problem for the users of Bitcoin. In fact, Bitcoin tried to introduce a solution known as BitcoinXT, which expanded the capabilities of their blocks, but the public outcry against this new operating system was enough for the plans to fall through.

Another internal problem that Bitcoin faces is the fact, that they are the first cryptocurrency of their class. This makes them a prototype, rather than a business, that can move forward with confidence, that the technology behind their operation is legitimate and sound. Bitcoin's function as a prototype that is trying to operate as a business is proving to be a bit tricky, as it is obvious that prototypes are usually tweaked or even completely redone before they are moved to their final point of maturation. This speaks to the idea that perhaps there will be other iterations of cryptocurrency platforms, before the public will feel as if they are in a position to move to a world, that operates only on cryptocurrency. The question of whether or not a prototype can become a viable product is still up in the air; however, it is common knowledge, that bitcoin is extremely close to finding itself in a position, where it will no longer be able to accommodate the number of people, who are seeking to exchange currency on its network.

One final problem with Bitcoin that does not have to do with blockchain is the rate of its money creation. As it stands right now, about half of bitcoin's currency includes currency, that has been around since the company's creation. Even though Bitcoin's users seem to be increasing in quantity, the rate at which the network is making money is extremely slow in comparison. There is more money being circulated into the network, but it's at a slower rate than is sustainable. In fact, some studies suggest that by the year 2025, Bitcoin currency will be a completely fixed money supply, meaning that there will be no new money moving into the network at all. If more and more users keep joining the network, but the money supply stays constant, it's likely that the users will start hoarding their money and this will conclude the exchange of funds within bitcoin.

As you can see from the plethora of examples, that were provided above, Bitcoin has a variety of issues, that it needs to fix, that has nothing to do with the blockchain technology within it. This means that blockchain technology has largely surpassed the ability of the bitcoin application itself. It may seem surprising, that the blockchain technology has become more useful than the application, that started it in the first place, but hopefully from the examples that were provided above, you can see that blockchain has very little to do with the problems that bitcoin is currently experiencing. Now that this has been established, we are going to look at how blockchain has been able to be implemented in ways that go beyond its first use within Bitcoin. Of course, it's important to understand, that even though there are problems within Bitcoin, there are still plenty of advantages to using this type of cryptocurrency mechanism, that we have highlighted through the discussion of how blockchain works. Even though Bitcoin is considered to be a prototype and there are flaws within its system, the advantages that Bitcoin can provide including network transparency and fairness should not be understated.

Moving Beyond Bitcoin: Fintech

Now that it's been established that bitcoin serves as a prototype for digital currency, the next step is to look at how the technology, that bitcoin started has infiltrated into other aspects of the technology. This will involve a discussion of fintech. Fintech, as the name suggests, stands for Financial Technology. Broadly, Fintech can be defined as any form of technology that focuses on expanding the capabilities of financial technology. Obviously, a great example of fintech at work is Bitcoin. Prior to Bitcoin, there was no viable form of cryptocurrency on the market. It's extremely important to understand that the development of Bitcoin is not, what exclusively led to the rise in fintech popularity. Instead, it was the development of blockchain technology that has provided fintech with the ability to flourish.

In addition to Bitcoin, other types of emerging forms of fintech include innovations in financial education and literature, innovations in the operations of bank branches, and innovations in investment procedures. While the capabilities of fintech were relatively small prior to the technology boom in the early 2000s, the internet revolution has caused fintech to explode. At its core, the goal of fintech is to provide greater ease of use across all financial technology platforms. Currently, there are many startup companies, that are dedicated to providing optimal fintech to its users. As the user-ability of apps continue to enhance society's ability to easily navigate the marketplace, there are a growing number of companies, that are interested in getting in on the action. Let's take a look at some of the most viable companies in fintech at the moment.

Fintech Company 1: Adyen

Adyen's primary location is in Amsterdam, where it has become a leading competitor in e-commerce payments. Some of the companies with which Adyen works with includes the ranks of Facebook, Airbnb, Netflix, Spotify, and Uber. It's more than likely that you have made a payment through at least one of these services, if not multiple services. From the perspective of blockchain, it's safe to say that Adyen has been able to overcome the problems, that Bitcoin still faces today, primarily the problem of not being able to accommodate for its vast user base. Adyen offers its customers ease of use through single-screen and single-click payment capabilities, as well as being able to offer mobile payments as well. If you've ever noticed that you have the option of storing your credit card information on a particular application so that you can easily purchase something without having to retype your credit card number into the page multiple times, you can thank Adyen for that as well.

Fintech Company 2: Bitnation

Bitnation takes the concepts that come with blockchain and more important decentralization a bit further through the design of an online society, that includes a digital government. The ideals of Bitnation suggest that one day, we could live in a world, where there is no physical government. The name of this digital government is known as Pangea. Prior to the development of Bitnation, there had never been an attempt for a nation to operate autonomously from a physical counterpart. So far, Bitnation has been able to digitally create and legalize within their nation the following types of documents and ceremonies:

1. Marriages
2. World Citizenships
3. Birth Certificates
4. Land Titles
5. Refugee IDs
6. Public Notary Documents

These types of documents that have been able to be verified within Bitnation bring up an important point about the abilities of blockchain. Blockchain is about verifying the ownership of something more than it is about the exchange of currency. This brings up the point that blockchain allows for the exchange of ownership in information in addition to the exchange of currency.

Fintech Company 3: Chain

The last fintech company at which we're going to look is known as Chain. This company works with leading credit card companies and financial institutions to create blockchain-based digital networks. You can interpret Chain as providing a service for the banks, who are worried that the future of banking may be decentralized in nature. Companies that are currently involved with Chain include the likes of Capital One, Visa, Citi, and Fidelity, just to name a few. This type of participation from the third-party banking institutions can be a bit troubling to some, because of the fact that these global conglomerations have already been known to be corrupt in nature. If they are having a private company build blockchain networks for them, doesn't this mean that the network is still going to be privatized, but on a digital platform? If the miners within these companies are basically virtual bank tellers, it seems to some people that the authenticity of the blockchain method diminishes.

As you can see from the examples above, the development of blockchain has given countless companies the ability to expand the breadth of their operations and also are able to provide the public with an easier way of purchasing goods and services. Who doesn't love how easy it is to simply click a button and have something be "paid"? Of course, this type of ease comes with its own set of problems for the user, who perhaps spends too much money on material goods, but these days everything seems to be about consumerism. Hopefully this chapter has provided you with important information about what Bitcoin is seeking to improve and companies known as fintech companies have taken the example of Bitcoin and have sought to avoid Bitcoin's mistakes as they pursue blockchain-dominated networks of their own. Unfortunately for Bitcoin, they may have missed the mark on how to create a flawless blockchain network, but for the rest of the technological world, Bitcoin invented something that was completely valuable and potentially priceless. Too bad Bitcoin didn't put a patent on their blockchain idea, before it changed everything.

Chapter 6: Ethereum, Smart Contracts, and Currency Creation

Now that you have a broad understanding of what fintech is and the ways in which it's currently being integrated into our society, we are now going to look at another type of blockchain technology, that is also increasing in popularity. This network is known as Ethereum. Ethereum is a bit like Bitcoin in the sense that individuals can trade currency with one another, but it also differs from Bitcoin in multiple ways. As you will see after reading this chapter, it appears as if Ethereum has combined the concepts of Bitcoin and other types of fintech such as Bitnation in order to bring a unique application to the market. Let's take a look at what Ethereum is, and how it expands upon other fintech applications that we've already discussed.

What is Ethereum?

Ethereum provides people with the opportunity to create their own blockchain networks. These blockchain networks can be completely customized, to provide you with a feeling of truly being in control of what's going on. To provide you with more detail about the capabilities of Ethereum, here is a list of what users can do with the application once they've decided that they want to build their own blockchain network:

1. Create and run their own markets
2. Document and keep track of debts or money owed
3. Fulfill requests that have been documented in wills or death documents
4. Create contracts with other people that serve as a legitimate proof of ownership

5. Create their own currency. This means that you can either use the currency that is inherent to Ethereum, which is called Ether, or you have the freedom to be able to denominate your currency in any way that you see fit.

In addition to these five capabilities, Ethereum also states that their application will be able to accommodate for any other types of advancements that are made within blockchain in the future. This declaration proves that even Ethereum believes that we have not reached our full potential with blockchain, and that this technology is likely to become even more useful in the future.

Ethereum and Smart Contracts

Another aspect of Ethereum is that, when you're building and operating a blockchain network on its system, you're also able to write and exchange your own Smart Contracts. The notion of a Smart Contract began all the way back in 1994, and when the idea was first conjured, the main goal was to eliminate the need to go to a physical location, when a process that required a lot of paperwork was being completed. For example, if you have ever bought a house, then you know that there are many steps that need to be completed, before you can say that you own the house outright. In addition to requiring many steps, buying a home also requires that you sign a lot of paperwork. This process can be tedious, and it can sometimes be difficult to coordinate the signing of all the paperwork, if you're a busy person. Use of a Smart Contract would seek to eliminate the process of physically meeting with someone to sign over the rights of the home. This means that instead of meeting with lawyers, realtors and the previous homeowners on the day, that you are finally ready to sign off on the rights to the home, this paperwork could instead be done remotely via a Smart Contract. Using blockchain parameters similar to the hash functions, that we have already discussed, the Smart Contract would know, when all of the requirements for the contract have been completed, and the Contract would not change hands until all of these requirements were met.

In addition to giving people the capability to exchange goods without physically interacting with one another, a Smart Contract also enables the possibility of ensuring the Contracts are being fulfilled in the most efficient way possible. For example, let's say that you're a landlord, who decides that you're going to use Ethereum in order to keep track of all of the leases with which you have to deal. You own an apartment complex, so you have a lot of leases that need to be monitored. Let's say that all of lease contracts require that your tenants pay you via Venmo (another blockchain application). All of your tenants are required to pay you their rent on the first of each month, as stated in your Contract with them. June 1st rolls around, and most of your tenants pay you on-time; however, there are 3 tenants, who are late with their payment. As a landlord, you know that it's a hassle to have to hunt these late tenants down and demand their rent payment. When you implement Smart Contracts, you don't have to hunt down anyone ever. Let's say that June 5th comes and you are still missing rent from these 3 irresponsible tenants. By setting a parameter within the blockchain Smart Contract network, the Contract will trigger that these three particular leases are in violation of their contract. The Contract will then demand a late payment within the tenant's wallet, and they will *automatically* be charged an additional fee for being late, and this will be tacked onto, what they currently owe you. This ensures greater fulfillment of all of the parameters of the Smart Contract, with very little effort on the part of the landlord, or Smart Contract administrator.

The Main Advantages of Ethereum and Smart Contracts

Ethereum enables people to access the advantages of Smart Contracts more easily, and there are two main advantages that exist, when people are using Smart Contracts. The first advantage is the idea of efficiency. As we saw in the example with the landlord, it can sometimes be difficult to obtain rent from tenants. Additionally, it can be even harder to receive late payments from tenants, especially when their account is not directly linked to yours and they have to agree to pay you the additional late fee in question. Even though late payments are definitely an inconvenience to a tenant, they are in place in the contract for a reason. If this parameter is in the contract, it means that the landlord is entitled to this fee, if the situation arises. Thus, Smart Contracts ensure that adequate monitoring of the contract that's in place at all times. Through blockchain algorithms, the Smart Contract is effectively able to watch the contract, even when you are not personally around to make sure that the contract is being properly followed.

The second advantage that a Smart Contract can provide on Ethereum is transparency. Let's stick to the example of the landlord with the tenants. With a Smart Contract, the actionable items within it are going to be accessible for both the tenant wallet and the landlord wallet. This means that the parameters of the contract are going to be clearly definable and easy to understand. This transparency makes it impossible for a tenant to claim that he or she did not know that there was a late fee attached to a particular portion of the contract. While transparency is certainly an advantage for the example that we just provided, one critique of the Smart Contract has to do with a lack of privacy. For example, if instead of a landlord lease the Smart Contract was a will, it may not necessarily be beneficial for the contract to be completely public in nature. This is an ongoing critique of the concept of a Smart Contract, and it's safe to say that this critique may become resolved in the future; however, the exact resolution is largely unknown at this point.

Chapter 7: The Future of Fintech and Blockchain Networks

As you have seen from the previous chapter as well as from the other chapters in this book, there are countless ways that blockchain is expanding and infiltrating the daily lives of members of society. Additionally, it's easy to see how blockchain is influencing financial operations; however, the manifestation of Smart Contract technology also makes it apparent that the future of digital contracts may also be on the horizon. Blockchain could potentially change the way that people interact with their physical environment. There are other types of technology that exists and is currently still being tested (such as the capabilities of virtual reality (VR). These types of innovations make fintech and blockchain extremely relevant. This chapter will look at the future of where these types of technology could potentially take humanity.

The Future of Technology and Fintech

As it stands now, one of the factions of society that is most excited about the future of blockchain technology is Wall Street. One of the biggest complaints that professional stock investors have has to do with the time, that it takes to exchange money internationally. It often takes weeks for foreign money to show up in an account, and these transactions are often expensive. This means that the amount of money that is being sent internationally is never the same amount that the receiver of the money actually sees when the transaction is finally completed, because of the foreign transaction fees that are related to this process. This is only one of the many reasons why Wall Street is attracted to the idea of the blockchain. It's obvious that Wall Street is loaded with money. When people with money have an idea or a curiosity, this ultimately means that they take action.

Enterprises such as IBM, Santander, and even Goldman Sach's have all developed Blockchain networks to test their reliability when exchanging money internationally. It's important to understand that when Bitcoin was first introduced to the public, the big banks and other entities often considered Bitcoin to only be relevant for people like drug dealers, illegal weapon traders, and individuals, who participated in the porn industry. For quite some time, no one really gave Bitcoin acknowledgement of its true potential and value, and instead associated it mostly with being a facilitator for illegal activity. This is no longer the case. Even though blockchain relies on the open sourcing of information in order to work, banks have finally come to realize that this does not mean that private information necessarily needs to be made public. At this point, plenty of algorithms have been developed, that prove that blockchain can uphold the integrity of private information. There is also an abstract reason why bankers are becoming interested in blockchain. This abstract reason is trust. Bankers know that trust is a pillar in any capitalist society, and they also know that the global public has a diminished sense of trust for their banks on a large scale. Stock market professionals are seeing blockchain as an opportunity to possibly gain the trust back that they have recently lost. We will have to wait to see if this trust is something that can be reobtained.

Blockchain Potential within the Government

In February 2017, the Republic of Georgia became the first national government to use the blockchain methodology in order to authorize transactions, that relate to property acquisition within the country. This is the first time that any national government has committed itself to using blockchain in a reputable way, so it's obviously big news for anyone who is interested in the future of blockchain. The official declaration of the Republic of Georgia states that it will now use blockchain to register new land titles, facilitate the purchasing and selling of land, approving the demolishing of land, provide notary services, and aid in the acquisition of mortgages or rental properties. What's more is that, while even though the Republic of Georgia is the first nation to take this tangible step towards the digital procurement of land, they are far from the only ones, who have thought about it. As of 2017, Sweden, Honduras and the County of Cook in Chicago, Illinois have also started to look into how they can use blockchain to make the processes within their municipalities more efficient.

A Final Word on Blockchain

Even though the Republic of Georgia is only one example of a small step that's been taken towards societal blockchain integration, this event can cause you to pause and wonder about the future of how nations will interact with one another in the future. If we use our imagination, it is not so far-fetched to think that perhaps one day most of our information and money will be taking up digital rather than physical space. If there does come a day when cryptocurrency becomes more valuable than physical money, does this mean that wars will be fought through hacking rather than through traditional warfare? This question is a small example of the imaginative questions that can arise when you begin to think about, where blockchain can possibly take us. This makes it obvious that technology can, at least for the time being, endlessly evolve the world in which we live.

While it's always fun to think creatively about the future, it's also important to seriously ponder the risks that are associated with blockchain implementation. As it stands right now, the biggest risks that can be linked to blockchain include insurance risks, bitcoin value, and figuring out how to regulate it. If it ever gets to a point where blockchain is considered to be an exclusive technology, this may not guarantee that insurance companies will agree to cover blockchain-supported endeavors right away. Additionally, the fact that the value of cryptocurrency can be determined by the owner of the currency can be a potential problem because there is no clear form of standardization for the currency right now. This problem is similar to the problem that some international economists are currently trying to solve regarding whether or not there should be the same type of currency globally. Lastly, regulation questions are probably the questions that pose the biggest risk for the future of blockchain. As with any type of budding technology or capitalist venture, the government is going to want its share. The government is also going to want to be able to watch over, who is using blockchain, in the hope of making sure, that it is being used in only legal ways. Even though the future is bright for blockchain, that is not to say that there are not serious risks associated with the technology that still have to be thought over and contemplated. For now, we can be happy for the progress that we have seen thus far.

Conclusion

Thank for making it through to the end of ***Blockchain - The Complete Guide to Blockchain Technology and How it is Creating a Revolution***. Hopefully, this book has taught you a lot about blockchain technology and its capabilities in a comprehensive and understandable manner. As you can see from reading this book, blockchain methodology has led to the development of countless applications that are extremely popular in today's society, including Airbnb, Netflix, and even Venmo. It is obvious that blockchain has made many technological advancements possible, and it's safe to say, that it will continue to do so in the future. The possibility of living in a completely digital world could possibly become a reality because of blockchain. The fact that we live in an age, where this might be possible is remarkable.

The next step is to keep doing research on the topic of blockchain in order to achieve any goal, that you may have regarding the technology. Maybe you are interested in building your own blockchain network, and have used this book as a jump-off point to gain knowledge on the subject. Maybe instead of starting your own blockchain network, you're looking to invest in shares of companies, that are starting projects via blockchain. If this is the case, the next step would be to do some research into the cost of these shares, before meeting with a broker, who can guide you in the right direction from an investment standpoint. Regardless of the reason why you are interested in blockchain, you should look next to gain even more insight into the subject, and how you accomplish this will depend on what your unique goals are with the knowledge you've been given.

Finally, if you found this book useful in any way, a review on Amazon is always appreciated!

www.ingramcontent.com/pod-product-compliance
Lightning Source LLC
Chambersburg PA
CBHW071033050326
40689CB00014B/3633